FUNDING OPTIONS
FOR
SMES & START UPS

Copyright © 2018
Eric Osei, Dr. Gordon Adomdza
& Lambert Nyabe

ISBN: 978-9988-2-7376-7

The CIP catalogue record for this book is available
from the George Padmore Research Library –
Ghana National Bibliography

Editing/Proofreading by
Hetura Books

Cover and Layout design by
Isaac Clad (Clad Impressions)

FUNDING OPTIONS FOR SMES & START UPS

Eric Osei, Dr. Gordon Adomdza
& Lambert Nyabe

THIS BOOK IS DEDICATED TO MY SON,
ANDREW KWABENA OSEI, AND EVERY
ENTREPRENEUR GLOBALLY.

ACKNOWLEDGEMENT

"O Lord who lends me life; lend me a heart replaced with thankfulness."

– Shakespeare

I thank God for this gift of writing. We owe it all to Him alone. To my co-authors, Dr. Gordon Adomdza and Lambert Nyabe; it has been a wonderful experience doing this project with you.

I also thank my wife, Cassandra, and our son, Andrew Osei. God bless you with every grace to identify your purpose.

To my partners and friends in the Netherlands, Africa in Motion, we are in this together; the team at Hetura Books for the editing and printing; and Clad Impressions for the cover design and layout; you guys are simply awesome.

To my partners and friends in the Netherlands, Africa in Motion, we are in this together; the team at Hetura Books for the editing and printing; and Clad Impressions for the cover design and layout; you guys are simply awesome.

CONTENTS

Acknowledgement v

Introduction vii

CHAPTERS

1 *Business Lifecycle* 1

2 *Creating Your Own Hockey Stick* 31

3 *Innovating Your Business Model for Investment* 39

4 *Developing Your Pitch Deck* 47

5 *Other Funding Options* 57

INTRODUCTION

Business funding in any economic climate can be challenging; whether you're looking for start-up funds, capital to expand, or money to hold on through the tough times. But given the current state of affairs, securing funds is as tough as ever. To help you find the money you need, we have compiled a guide on the different funding options for SMEs and startups that you should know.

Notwithstanding most business owners use their own cash or savings to initially fund their startup operations, many of them may need an injection of additional capital from an external source at some point. With more financing options becoming available to small-business owners seemingly every day, the funding landscape is constantly evolving.

SMEs play an important economic role in almost every country. In many African countries, for example, the SME sector contributes a substantial number of new jobs. Despite the significant role of SMEs to most African economies, they face the threat of failure as past statistics indicate that three out of five businesses fail within few years of starting. Some of the factors attributed to these failures include: lack of access to funding, unfavorable government policies, and, in some cases, the capacity of the SMEs themselves.

In Ghana, readily available data on SMEs is scarce but statistics from the Registrar-General's Department suggests that 92 per cent of companies registered are micro, small, and medium enterprises. SMEs in Ghana have also been noted to provide about 85 per cent of manufacturing employment, contribute about 70 per cent to Ghana's GDP, and therefore have the catalytic impacts on economic growth, income, and employment.

SMEs are important players for national and international development; they are therefore important players to national and international development; whether one considers the situation of a developed or developing economy.

Aside being an important *source of employment* and income in many *developing countries*, SMEs, with their flexible nature, have a better adaptability to changing market conditions; this makes them better poised to withstand cyclical downturns. The dispersion of SMEs across the nation also promotes better distribution of income and generates additional value in raw materials and products even as they bring about efficiencies in domestic markets. They will, however, fail to achieve this without access to the right kinds of funding.

Again, SMEs that are able to access funding from local banks struggle to repay their loans. This is in no way favorable for the survival of SMEs in most countries. Bank lending rate in Ghana averaged 29.48 percent from 2005 until 2018, reaching an all-time high of 42.84 percent in July of 2016 and a record low of 21.24 percent in March of 2008 *(Source:wwww.tradingeconomics.com)*. Such rates don't support the growth and development of the SME sector in many African economies.

This book provides you with the needed guidance to make appropriate funding decisions concerning your business. Notable among key issues discussed include the different funding options available: debt, equity, angel investing and impact investments. Others include pitching new ideas versus growth stage ideas and developing your pitch deck.

We are excited that this material has finally been released to provide you with some information required in making the right decisions concerning your business funding needs.

CHAPTER ONE

BUSINESS LIFECYCLE

Lifecycle Intro

Everything that grows dies. That is the law of nature to govern living organisms. Businesses, like humans, grow and die. Hence, their existence is along a lifecycle. However, businesses can extend their lifespan at various points along their lifecycle. Some people pay attention to their health that they are able to live longer than the average life expectancy. This involves a strategic and often deliberate effort to sustain certain practices that extend their life. IBM is one of the oldest companies still relevant today. It seems to have been able to prolong its lifespan as it matured on its lifecycle. Today, IBM is leading research and discovery in new areas such as Artificial Intelligence and blockchain technology. Yet, its cousins such as Kodak and Nokia could not prolong their relevance on their lifecycle as they matured.

To sustain its lifespan at different parts of the lifecycle, a business needs the right resources from sources that are interested in that stage of its lifecycle. Businesses at the early stage need support from resource providers who strategically fund companies at the early stage and understand the risks involved. The same goes for the growth stage. Businesses at this stage have to approach a different set of resource providers who work at and understand the growth stage of the business lifecycle. Attempting to attract growth-type investors at the early stage could be a waste of time and a signal that the business does not understand their needs or the market.

When startups have clarity about their lifecycle and life span, it helps them develop and implement strategies better. As we have seen from above, looking for the right type of funding is important. A number of writers have come up with a few different categorizations of the funding space. In our research, we found that of [1]Frank Demmler who provided a very good template for structuring the funding landscape.

He notes that startups evolve through development stages before they become investible. As they evolve, the level of resources needed per stage also increases. Further,

---

1   Raising Money For New And Emerging Companies (https://bit.ly/2sCr11G) By

to be successful in raising subsequent funding, the startup needs to continually resolve uncertainty at each stage as investors consider the level of uncertainty as they compute a matrix perception of risk and reward. Different investors, generally classified into debt and equity, will make these calculations at each stage of the funding. Hence, being stage-conscious is important. We will, however, align different types of funders to the stages a little later. In the following, we dive a little deeper into the categories Demmler outlines.

Business Lifecycle

According to Demmler, a business typically has four lifecycle stages: Early, Growth, Maturity, and Decline. As noted earlier, if the business does not sustain itself, its performance eventually declines. Large corporations are of ten in the Maturity stage and implement strategies to sustain their lifespan at maturity. Startups are often at the Early stage and need to strategize to enter the Growth stage.

Further, as noted earlier, startups evolve at the Early stage into an investible venture. In the evolution, they go through multiple sub-stages. While different analysts and experts identify different numbers of steps for this early stage, Demmler identifies the following sub-stages: Idea, Feasibility, Verification, Demonstration, and Commercialization. Let's take these sub-stages in turns.

Frank Demmler

IDEA SUB-STAGE

The Idea sub-stage is the riskiest stage of the process. You may have heard that ideas are worth a dime. The notion here is that even the best ideas are difficult to invest in because the entrepreneur venturing on the idea may not be the right fit. It takes the right entrepreneur to develop the best idea into a business. Hence, investors are often wary of putting a lot of investment into this stage. From experience, investors are often more willing to invest in ideas at this stage if the ideas are groundbreaking and they believe they can muster enough control to take over the fate of their investment should something go bad. However, due to the dangers, entrepreneurs are only left with a few sources:

<u>Sweat Equity:</u> This is the resources (money and effort) that, you, the entrepreneur, put into the idea. Sweat equity is probably more about effort than money but it is an important resource that needs to be included in this discussion. Sweat equity is important because it signals to the investor who comes along later that you care enough about your idea. Hence, investors want to see that you have really expended your energy on the idea. You should really think about how to capture and show sweat equity. It is important that investors know that you have put your all into the business. There is nothing embarrassing about admitting that you have gone to bed on a hungry belly because you had to buy

supplies to finish a job or product for a customer. Investors want entrepreneurs to be transparent because investment is a partnership that requires trust and trust is more likely with transparency than without.

<u>Personal Funding:</u> This will include personal savings and debt. Personal savings will include any money that you had saved either in flexible or fixed deposits including retirement savings. Again, if you believe in the idea, you should be able to put in "your all" and go broke (as some investors will expect – others may have a different doctrine). Personal debt will involve small loans such as lines of credit or credit card debt. These are debt options you had because of your creditworthiness.

It pays to develop a good credit history. Credit worthiness metrics by funders may not make sense to some people but if that is how to build a credit history, it may be worth it. For instance, if a bank expects you to show the ability to take small loans and make timely repayments, then even if you could afford to not take a loan, it might make sense to take the loan and make the expected repayments to establish a credit history. Being credit worthy and qualifying for small loans could be one way of salvaging a business in times of need.

<u>Friends, Family and Fools:</u> You should be able to leverage your social capital at the early stages. The practice of leveraging social capital starts with being able to raise funding from friends, family and fools. Friends should be able to buy into your idea if they believe in it and trust your capabilities. Family will also provide funding; sometimes just to support you and not necessarily because they believe in the idea. Writers often identify a third category of funders referred to as "fools." It is believed these people are not friends or family but strangers who just happen to have an encounter with you and, for some reason, tend to believe in you or the idea enough to put money into the venture. The best imagery we heard for this is when the "fool" meets the entrepreneur and after a short interaction, says, "I want to invest in you; what's your idea?"

As an entrepreneur, you should learn to state your personal and entrepreneurial objectives clearly when you communicate with friends, family and strangers. It is better to be clear on the big picture. You should be able to state the main problem or the domain area of the problem. If you are interested in digital payments towards a cashless economy, you should find a very clear succinct way of communicating that to friends, family, and strangers at the least opportunity. When you are known for the big picture, it is easier for friends, family, and strangers to latch on to new ideas in that space and feel like they are contributing to solving the problem that you have always been passionate about.

<u>Government Programs And Industry Competitions:</u> Government programs will often provide grants to support startup ideas based on the objectives or focus of the funding program. For example, if the government wants to increase solar power adoption, it might have a grant program for startups that develop new products and applications in solar power generation and distribution. Grants can also come from competitions organized in certain sectors by non-governmental bodies. The goal will be similar: to foster innovation in specific spaces with the hope of promoting investible ventures in the future. You should scan your local environment for programs that are in line with your area of focus because grants are free funding for your dream.

You should, however, be careful not to chase funding that takes you away from your focus. If you have done research into a market and its customers and have come up with a unique perspective to drive your innovation, it is a bad strategy to chase free money that takes you away from that unique perspective. The funding could spring life into the team but waste your time in pursuing your objectives. In the long run, it will likely not be worth it.

Feasibility Sub-stage

The feasibility stage, according to Demmler, is where you conduct research on whether the venture has prospects. This is also a very risky stage. The research might show that the venture is not feasible for the market, either from an economic, market, or regulatory perspective. For instance, it may not be possible to source materials ethically to produce the product. Or privacy rules might not allow you to build the operational model needed to put the product on the market. Hence, funders who are more susceptible to this stage understand the risks involved.

It is fair to say that most of the funders or funding sources identified above will likely also support the feasibility stage. However, potential "new" funders coming in at this stage due to the promise of the idea stage may include equity investors such as the angel investor according to Demmler. It is important to distinguish an equity investor from a debt funder. Equity investors exchange the funding they provide with shares from the company and therefore participate in decision-making to safeguard their interest. Debt funders provide funding based on the availability of a tangible collateral (in rare cases they will give a loan based on the prospects of a receivable e.g. a lucrative and reliable purchase order from a customer).

Another look at the description of feasibility as a research phase by Demmler suggests that debt funders will not be able to participate at this stage since the product has not been outdoored on the market yet (you may still be able to raise debt by providing collateral without promise of receivables):

<u>Angel Investors:</u> Angel investors are typically wealthy individuals who normally made money as entrepreneurs. They are interested in new ideas, want to support innovation in specific areas of interest, and/or like the startup experience. If they were previously entrepreneurs, then it is likely they invest to relive the startup experience vicariously through the entrepreneur they are funding. They also make good returns as early investors if they get it right. Not all ventures at the feasibility stage will be attractive to angel investors.

Entrepreneurs should show angel investors how the angels get their investment back with dividends. Angels typically want three to five times of what they put in. They will typically get this return when a larger funder puts money into the venture and allows the angel to get three to five times of their investment and exit the investment arrangement.

For instance, if you got USD 50,000 at the feasibility stage, they expect three (USD 150,000) up to about five times (USD 250,000). Normally, the venture is not making so much money as to be able to pay the angel investor from profits. This is because even if they are making great profits, it's also a growth stage so they cannot afford to be paying huge sums out of their returns as dividends. They need to put the money back into the venture to finance the growth. Hence, the angel investor has to wait for a larger funder to appear so they can cash out. The implication is that venture has to have a real growth need for an angel investor to be attracted to it. The need has to be such that when it is filled, the venture will be attractive to a funder much larger than the angel investor in terms of their funding value.

At Demmler's feasibility stage, the interested angel investor is probably motivated by the prospects of the research outcomes since the product is not on the market yet. This means the angel is coming in a bit early and will have to stay on for a few more stages before he/she can exit the arrangement.

Entrepreneurs should be able to impress the investors by showing that they are capable of growing the venture rapidly to be attractive to a larger funder. If the angel investor does not sense this capability on your part, then it may not matter how great the idea is, he or she may not invest. Hence, angel investor pitches should not only focus on the idea but also on the capability of the team or your ability to attract talent you currently don't have to fill any gaps.

VERIFICATION SUB-STAGE

According to Demmler, the verification stage entails a "quiet" release of the prototype of the product onto the market for research purposes. This stage allows you to conduct more market tests while building the go-to-market team. It is basically the stage where you test the venture's business model to understand the value chain that will deliver the product to the broader market. Hence, verification may involve sales to early adopter groups in the market who are excited about the product because it is new and provides an interesting perspective not necessarily because it works extremely well. They are therefore willing to be patient with you and provide the necessary feedback that allows you to get the product ready for the broader market.

According Demmler, by the verification stage, you will likely have exhausted your personal funding and are not likely able to participate at this stage. You will therefore likely rely on angel investors and government programs that provide sizable funding for this stage. We believe there are other potential funding which allows you to finance inventory even if a small number of early adopters are being served.

Demonstration Sub-stage

According to Demmler, the demonstration stage is where the venture outdoors the product and repeatable sales process is established. It is also where the management team is ready for the next stage. Finding a repeatable sales process means a lot of interaction with customers and a market research to understand how to fulfill customer preferences as well as understand the business model enough to replicate it when the product is put on the market on a larger scale.

Demmler identifies angel investment as the only funding source at the demonstration stage. We think there are other types of funding that can provide financing for production to provide a more effective market test. Here are three likely ones:

<u>Crowdfunding:</u> These days, entrepreneurs can use crowdfunding to raise funding at the early stage, probably more applicable at the demonstration sub-stage of the early stage. Entrepreneurs can use gift-based or equity-based crowdfunding. However, at the idea stage, you are more likely to be successful with gift-based crowdfunding. Gift-based crowdfunding is when you launch an idea or concept on a crowdfunding site and offer the delivery of the product or service and other souvenirs in return for donations. This is a great way of funding inventory.

If you get USD 20 per donation from 100 people for a product that costs USD 15 to produce and ship, there are three things happening here: You have cash advantage by raising production and inventory finance before supplying the product; you have better sense of how much to produce since you are basically producing to order; finally, you are also able to cut out the middle man and supply directly to the customer. Gift-based crowding therefore becomes a great way of raising funding for products, allowing you to receive money to fund inventory before supplying.

<u>Microloans or Small Business Loans:</u> As an entrepreneur, you may be able to get small loans at this stage if you show good traction or have good collateral. In rare cases, showing reliable receivables may get you loans to finance the delivery of products.

If possible, you should explore loans for funding operations and inventory instead of equity which requires you to part with some ownership of the company. The best situations for possibility is when the venture has a really strong cashflow. If ventures are great and can easily service a loan while also growing, then such a venture may not need equity investment. That may not be the case if such a venture also needs to grow rapidly. Loans may not be able to finance such rapid growth.

<u>Internal Funding:</u> There are also a number of ways of raising money internally to make business run efficiently especially with an increasing interest in the product at the demonstration sub-stage. In no particular process or category, let us note two examples and illustrate how to raise funding to enable inventory before production and how to ensure you collect receivables or revenue in

efficient ways. Some of the ways of financing inventory include arranging for a 60-day or 90-day grace period with suppliers so that you can loan inputs to make the product for customers, get revenue, and pay suppliers before 60 or 90 days.

You can also use subscription to raise inventory finance by asking customers to subscribe to the product in advance. In terms of efficient collection of receivables, you can use methods such as factoring. Factoring enables you to take the invoices you have issued to the customers that have received the product (or receivables) and go sell to a funder at a discount. For instance, if ten customers owe you to the tune of USD 1,000, you can collect GHC 950 from a funder and on condition that the funder will be able to collect the full value of the GHC 1000 from customers.

COMMERCIALIZATION SUB-STAGE

The commercialization stage is when the venture is widely unveiled in the market with a strong repeatable set of value flows in its business model that delivers revenues over cost. At this point, most aspects of the business model have been tested and, therefore, risk and uncertainty is further reduced. Crowdfunding, debt and equity funding are all potentially relevant sources of funding at this stage.

According to Demmler, this stage is attractive to other types of equity funders who have more resources than the angel investor to provide funding to scale the business up and take the value proposition to its market potential. Larger funding allows the angel investor to make their expected funding returns and exit the relationship with you.

<u>Venture Capitalist:</u> Demmler introduced the Venture Capitalist (VC) at the demonstration stage but we provide a description of the funding type here. Unlike an angel investor who invests their own money, a VC is an investment manager who invests other people's money. This means that a VC is stricter with the venture and is more involved in decision-making to ensure that the venture keeps in line with the stated objectives. The VC expects about ten times (on average often makes about five times) how much they put in in a period of five to seven years (longer in times of economic downturn).

Just like the angel investor, the VC expects a big pay day when a much larger investor shows up to put much more into the venture. Normally, there will be institutional investors, a competitor of the venture who comes to merge with it, a buyer who wants to bring it in-house, a private placement or an initial public offering. These entities will typically raise much more, sometimes fifty times what the VC put in to grow the business to the stage where these larger investors are interested. Hence, the VC is able to achieve the ten times they expected.

For illustration, let's consider the VCs that invested in WhatsApp[2]. They would have expected ten times when they came in. It is easy to see how they indeed made good on their investment when Facebook bought WhatsApp for $19bn.

VCs normally invest large amounts of money (unless they are micro-VCs). This is because they often raise a large fund but operate as a small group of professional investor partners. As a result, the partners are not able to invest in a large number of companies because the larger the number, the more boards they have to sit on and the more decision variables they have to contend with. As such, entrepreneurs have to need a large amount of investment to attract a VC.

Also, the growth potential for the venture should be very high to allow for the kind of growth that will in turn attract the larger investors who will ensure that the VC gets the 10x they expect. Entrepreneurs should also be willing to trade control for shares when they accept VC funding. There have been cases where VCs have kicked out founders because they didn't think such founders could deliver the growth potential of the venture. Hence, you should be clear that you can evolve as a person as the venture evolves to the high growth stage where they attract a VC.

You should also be ready for value proposition and business model innovation at this point. High growth up the mainstream parts of the venture's target market will require some innovation as the venture approaches this stage from

---

2   Will be good to know one or two

start of its lifecycle. Most of the innovation here will be introduced by the VC and based on the market experience of their team of value chain innovators and may not rely so much on your learning and experience. Hence, you should really be psychologically ready to engage with VCs at this stage. One of the most impactful advice we have heard here is that entrepreneurs should think of VCs as entities that come to fund they, the entrepreneurs', dream.

Business Lifecycle and Funding Options

It has become apparent that for entrepreneurs to compete effectively in business, they must first be well abreast with the ever changing business environment. The business environment is always evolving and businesses go through different cycles throughout their life. Your ability as an entrepreneur to identify, nurture, and move to the next stage of the business life cycle can be very cumbersome. Most businesses, if not all, are established to grow and it is very important for you to identify the stage of your business, challenges and also put measures in place to excel in the business environment.

THE SEVEN STAGES OF THE BUSINESS LIFECYCLE AND SOURCES OF FUNDING

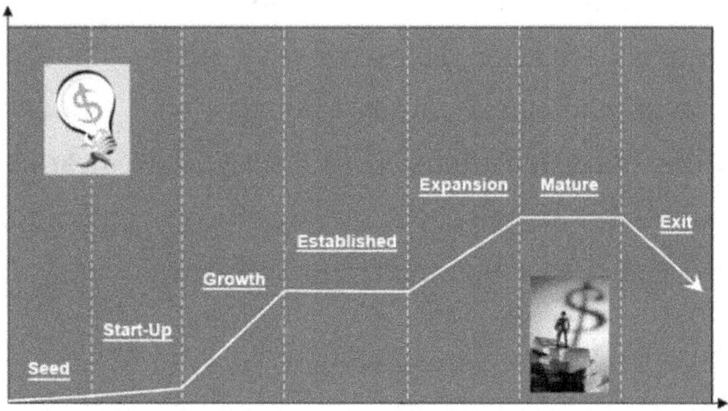

Source: http://blog.yellowpageskenya.com/the-7-stages-of-business-life-cycle/

1. Seed Stage

The seed stage of a business lifecycle is where you discover a gap or demand in the society and try to develop a product that meets the demand. Demmler referred to this stage as embryotic stage and identified five processes businesses go through at this level. The processes are ideation, feasibility, verification, demonstration, and commercialization.

IDEA

This is the stage where entrepreneurs identify a problem in the society and come up with ideas of solving it. The entrepreneur engages in a brainstorming section. Brainstorming session is very important at this stage;

whether you have few or many ideas. Questions like: what is it that is lacking in the society? How can it be solved? What are the various ways of solving it? This and many others are the starting point of developing a business idea. Your passion and commitment are the driving forces at this stage. You may not progress to the next stage if you get discouraged at this stage.

Taking note of ideas that come to mind is very important at this stage. It does not really have to be a perfect one. You just have to enumerate the ideas as many as possible as they come to mind. Also, you need not judge them; neither do they have to be arranged in any format.

FEASIBILITY

Feasibility study is an integral part of product development. It gives you the chance to explore and investigate whether the product to be developed will be profitable and viable. According to Bause et al (2016), feasibility studies aim to point out chances and risks of projects which are planned or already in process. They opined that there are five areas of feasibility studies: technical, economic, legal, operational, and scheduling. Some of the common methods used at this stage include, SWOT analysis, sensitivity and profitability analysis, and investment appraisal.

VERIFICATION

At each product development stage, you have to continue asking whether the right product is being designed. This helps in keeping track as the product is being designed to tackle a specific problem.

DEMONSTRATION

One of the surest ways of making the product known in the market for the first time is through demonstration. At this stage, you locate prospective customers and give them the product free of charge or at a reduced cost for testing. You then request for a genuine feedback from them to improve the product before commercializing it. Product demonstration provides visual support to enhance the quality of sales presentation. Visual or hands-on prospects often need to see the product in action to fully grasp its value and potential.

COMMERCIALIZATION

In this stage, the main problems of the business are obtaining customers and delivering the product or service contracted for. The products are fully launched and sent to the market. Introducing the new product into the market is a significant business achievement. The companies will have to overcome the challenge of market acceptance and pursue one niche opportunity. It is, therefore, not advisable to spread money and time resources too thin.

Funding Opportunities

Since businesses at this stage are only ideas, it is very difficult to secure huge funding. Most investors will not invest in the business at this stage. Therefore, the business has to rely on owners' savings, funds from friends, and family. This is because the business has no proven market or customers, and investors may not be willing to invest. The growing demand to curb the chronic unemployment in Africa has compelled most African governments to set up funds in the form of grant to support idea-stage businesses. These funds are very competitive as you have to compete with other entrepreneurs with brilliant ideas. Other potential sources include suppliers in the form of flexible credit terms and customers who make advance payment for their products to be delivered.

During the seed stage, the young company could readily prepare a five-year plan to convince new shareholders/resource providers to support the next phases of development. Introduction of the company and assessing the business model will often consume the equity invested by the owners. There are multitudes of good ideas when attempting to launch a company. To be successful, the young company will need visionary managers to dynamically adapt the business model to stay in line with rapid market evolution.

At this stage of the business the focus is on matching the business opportunity with your skills, experience, and passions. Other focal points include: deciding on a business ownership structure, finding professional advisors, and business planning. Jeff Bezos argued that if you do not understand the details of your business, you will fail. Hence, understanding the business model is very important at this stage.

2. Start-Up Stage

At this stage, you should know if the business idea is worth pursuing and if the product addresses the societal problem that was identified based on the feedback from the public (potential customers). The process can be reiterated till the product meets customers and market demand. The entrepreneur needs to learn and adjust the business model to ensure profitability and meet customers' expectations. The business can be set on the right track by adjusting the business model in meeting customers' and market demand.

At this point, you must register the company legally according to the company law of your country. This will give you leverage in the industry to compete effectively. The company can either be registered as a sole proprietorship, partnership or limited liability company. The type of company also influences the source of finance that you will seek as it would be very difficult for a sole proprietor to raise equity investment.

You must do a lot of research to really understand the market and the need of the customer. You must focus on putting the necessary structures like keeping record of your activities including financial records, a clear governance structure, chain of command, and a well-composed management team. A common feature of startups is loss-making at the early stage. You should not be discouraged when you experience losses at the early stage of your business development. You should rather analyze your financial results and put measures in place to improve your profitability.

Funding Opportunities

This stage is very important in the business life cycle. At this stage, some entrepreneurs think launching their product and registering their company is all they need to approach any investor for funds. They end up wasting all their time running around ignoring the most valuable things that have to be done to fully penetrate into the market. To access funds other than owner capital, friends, family, suppliers, customers, or grants, you have to put the business structures in place. Investors do not release funds just like that because it is their hard-earned money; as such, they make sure they conduct all the necessary due diligence before investing into any business.

One of the commonest investors to approach at this stage is angel investors. Angel investors are wealthy individuals who invest in start-up and growth businesses in return for an equity stake. The investment can involve both time and money depending on the investor. These individuals are prepared to take high risks in the hope of high returns. As a result, angel investors' finance can be expensive for the business.

It is not advisable for startups or companies at early growth stage to have high level of gearing. Securing loan from banks at this stage can be very expensive as the banks will charge high interest rate because of the risk they are taking. The riskier a business, the more return investors will require. Startups are considered to be very risky as it is difficult to forecast future cash flow with any degree of certainty. However, if you are able to secure a loan for your business at this stage, you must keep in touch with the lenders/bank. You must service the loan regularly. You should feel free to approach your bankers as early as possible if you find it difficult to pay back the loan. Usually, banks are ready to have discussions with their clients on repayment of the loan. Some banks go to the extent of freezing the interest on the loan and waiving the penal charges attached to the loan on maturity when the client has liquidity issues. This can only happen when the client maintains good relationship with the bank.

3. Growth Stage

The business has endured the initial stages of the business lifecycle and is currently in its growth. The business begins to generate revenue and new customers. This recurring revenue will help pay for your operating expenses and open up new business opportunities. Currently, your business could be operating at a net loss or maintaining a healthy profit, but there could be some competition. This is also when you need to fine tune your business model and implement proven methodologies, sales models, marketing models, and operational models before expanding your venture for the mass market.

The biggest challenge growth companies face is dealing with the constant range of issues bidding for more time and money. Effective management is required and a possible revised business plan. The entrepreneur learns to train and delegate to conquer this stage of development.

The management has to focus on running the business in a more formal way to deal with the increased sales and customers. It is also very important to improve accounting and management systems to keep track of the finances of the company. One of the mistakes most business owners make at this stage is hiring unqualified family members and friends to manage the business. This, most at times, ruins the business because this is the stage that the business faces stiff competition and needs qualified people to deal with the influx of business.

SOURCES OF FUNDING

Sources of funding at this stage include bank loans, grant, and leasing. It is worth noting that the use of retained earnings, that is, ploughing back of profits, cannot be overemphasized. This boosts the company as the funds are readily available for management to use in consultation with shareholders. Business owners can also enter into partnerships with entities or individuals who share in the ideas of the company. Companies with great social impact will succeed in raising funds from impact investors.

4. Established Stage

The business has been a thriving company and established its presence in the industry at this stage. It has now reached the stage where it is ready to expand and spread its roots into new markets and distribution channels. With this, the business will experience a rapid growth in revenue and cash flow. The established stage takes advantage from the proven sales model, marketing model, and operations model set forth from your growth stage.

It is far too easy to rest on the success during this life stage; the marketplace is relentless and competitive, and management has to stay focused on the bigger picture. Issues like the economy, competitors or changing customer tastes can quickly end all that the company has worked for. An established lifecycle company will be focused on improvement and productivity. To compete in an established market, you will require better business practices along with automation and outsourcing to improve productivity.

Funding Opportunities

The sources of funding include profit, banks, investors and government grant.

5. Expansion Stage

This lifecycle stage is characterized by a new period of growth into new markets and distribution channels. To start capitalizing on the success of the business, the management will need to capture a larger market share and find new revenue stream. This stage is often the choice of the small business owner to gain a larger market share and find new revenue and profit channels. This requires intense research and development as the business moves into new markets.

The focus should be on businesses that complement your existing experience and capabilities. The strategy to pursue at this stage is to develop new products or services to existing markets or expand existing business into new markets and customer type. Moving into unrelated areas can be disastrous.

Funding Opportunities

The sources of funding include banks, licensing/ franchising, new investors, joint ventures and partners.

6. Mature Stage

Year over year sales and profits tend to be stable, however competition remains fierce. Eventually sales start to fall off and a decision is needed whether to expand or exit the company. Businesses in the mature stage of the lifecycle will be challenged with dropping sales, profits, and negative cash flow. The biggest issue is how long the business can support a negative cash flow. This could be the time to move back to the expansion stage or move on to the final life cycle stage, that is, to exit. It is important to search for new opportunities and business ventures. Management can effectively focus on means of reducing costs and find ways to sustain cash flow through increasing revenue.

It is important for businesses to avoid overtrading at this stage. Overtrading happens when businesses try to do too much too quickly with too little long-term capital; so that it is trying to support too large a volume of trade with the financial resources at its disposal. Even if the business operates at a profit at this stage during overtrading, it could easily run into serious trouble because it will be short of cash and this will move the business to the last stage of the business lifecycle.

Other factors that may end small companies too quickly include changes in the economy, society and market conditions.

Funding Opportunities

The sources of funding include banks, licensing/franchising, new investors, joint ventures and partners and government grant.

7. Exit Stage

This is the big opportunity for your business to cash out on all the effort and years of hard work or it can mean shutting down the business. The business has to look at the possible exit strategies available and choose the best one that works for them. Both business merges and acquisitions require realistic valuation. At times the company can be overvalued and this favors shareholders willing to sell their share. It may have been years of hard work to build the company, but think about the real value in the current marketplace. If the management decides to close your business, the challenge is to deal with the financial and psychological aspects of a business loss. The management has to look at the business operations and competitive barriers to make the company worth more to the buyer. It will be prudent to set up legal buy-sell agreements along with a business transition plan. It is also important to consult financial advisers for the best tax strategy for selling or closing out the business.

Each stage of the business lifecycle may not occur in chronological order. Some businesses will be "built to flip," quickly going from startup to exit. Others will choose to avoid expansion and stay in the established stage.

Whether the business is a glowing success or a dismal failure depends on the ability of the management team to adapt to its changing lifecycles. What one focuses on and overcomes today will change in the future. Understanding where the business fits in lifecycle will help the management to foresee upcoming challenges and make the best business decisions.

CHAPTER TWO

CREATING YOUR OWN HOCKEY STICK

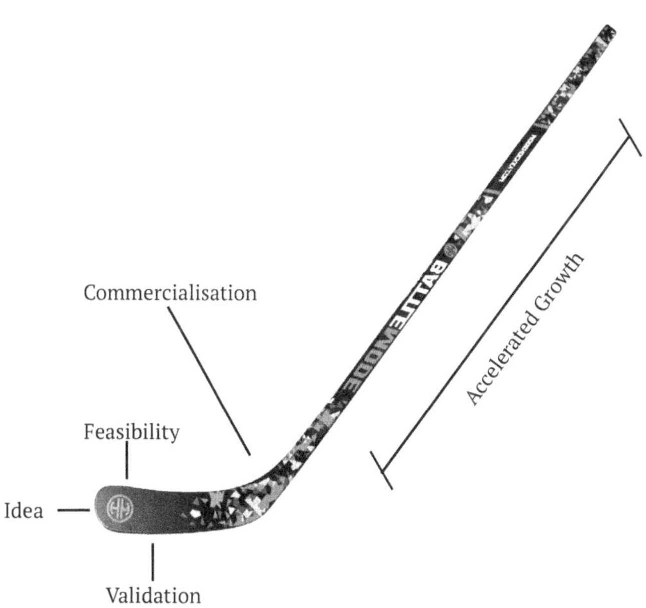

The hockey stick is used to describe the growth prospects of a venture. It's important that the imagery is not a slanted baseball bat but a hockey stick and that is because the horizontal blade part is supposed to represent the sub-stages we described early on: idea, feasibility, validation and commercialization.

Commercialization starts an inflexion point in the stick that leads to an accelerated growth up to the handle and beyond. In his book, Bobby Martin, author of *The Hockey Stick Principles: The Four Key Stages to Entrepreneurial Success*[3] provides more information on the stages of the hockey stick growth – a good read for all.

Hockey stick growth prospects are good news for investors! It tells an angel investor that they can get the 3x they expect. It tells the VC that they can get the 10x they expect. It gives confidence to the post-VC funding analysts that equity investors will have a clean exit and therefore should be encouraged to invest.

Entrepreneurs need to be able to show their venture is a hockey stick venture. If it's not, they should be ready to innovate their value proposition and/or business model to get the hockey stick growth projections.

---

3   https://bit.ly/2JEwgYu

High Growth Ventures

Most traditional funding discussions, especially those involving equity investors, typically focus on high growth ventures because they ensure a payday for the equity investor. However, not all ventures need to be high growth. Some need to grow slowly. For instance, a new kind of service that requires skills training and experience of the service providers may need to grow slowly and not rapidly. Not all sectors can have high growth ventures and for some cultures or consumer markets, customers may expect certain types of brands to grow slowly and not rapidly.

Low growth ventures like small businesses that do not scale rapidly are not of interest to the equity investor because it will take too long to get their returns. Hence, entrepreneurs working with low growth models are often advised to focus on debt or other creative funding models that allows them to grow slowly. For instance, with good cashflow, a small business can take a loan and pay back in installment. This funding model will work for slow growth. The moment the venture needs to grow rapidly and needs large tranches of funding, often with a certain level of risk, debt funding may be equally too risky as a financing option with a much larger collateral at stake.

It should however be noted that when small businesses have perfected their model, developed it into a repeatable turnkey model that others can replicate, they may be ready for scale and therefore larger debt or equity investment. Equity investors may be interested in a successful restaurant that wants to have multiple locations or a retail service, such as microfinance or real estate shop that wants to go nationwide.

SCALABILITY AND OPERATING LEVERAGE

Another important factor to discuss in terms of growth is scale. Scale is important in funding because scalability ensures the rapid growth trajectory on the market and cannot typically be achieved with profits. Scalability determines the hockey stick shape. If a venture is scalable, it likely needs external funding. A successful venture can grow internally through marketing and expanding its product line without additional outside funding. However, most scale scenarios require a larger infusion of funding than can be arranged internally. Hence, understanding what scaling means and how an investor sees it is important.

Analysts suggest that investors will look out for "operating leverage" to determine if the venture is scalable.

Alex Taussig, writing in *Fortune Magazine*[4] describes operating leverage as such: "If you add operating costs (sales, marketing, administrators, R&D, etc.) at the same rate you grow revenue, then your business does not scale. Alternatively, if additional revenue requires relatively

---

4   https://for.tn/2JA5RuR

smaller and smaller additions to operating costs, then congratulations… your business scales!"

Essentially, businesses that experience proportional increase in costs and make revenue cannot achieve a healthy hockey stick projection. "Healthy" is the word here in that the venture can grow wildly but without operating leverage, that growth is not a scaling growth and will not return the 3x investment the angel investor put in or the 10x investment the VC wants.

Entrepreneurs should understand what scalability means. They should think of how to innovate revenue streams and cost structures to grow revenues faster than costs can respond.

SCALING STRATEGIES

Scaling strategies may also be of interest to the investor. The strategy you choose might align with your business model. However, what if that business model is not of interest to investors? Then, could the venture innovate to change your scaling strategy to attract investment? Anderson Dees and friends identified three key scaling strategies with respect to social impact[5]. However, we have found these strategies to provide a clear sense of the options in the space.

____

5   Dees, J. G., Anderson, B. B. and Wei-Skillern, J., 2004. Scaling Social Impact: Strategies for Spreading Social Innovations. Stanford Social Innovation Review, Spring,

The first is dissemination. From a social impact perspective, dissemination of product information or intellectual property to a wide audience or a set of users helps scale a solution quickly. However, for-profit companies can also use dissemination for marketing so that users will still need to pay to receive full value from the offering. Most investors may find this model too risky. However, some investors may find the role of dissemination for marketing quite interesting and be willing to explore funding for rather impactful ideas. The second is affiliation.

There is loose affiliation where the venture invites others in the value chain to collaborate to provide value and fulfil delivery to customers. Tight affiliation will involve the venture working more tightly with partners such as seen in franchising where there are certain controls around e.g. brand, pricing, sourcing, etc. Investors may find affiliation more interesting than dissemination, especially franchising. Equity investors may fund scaling by franchising because if managed well, it can grow the business rapidly. Likewise, investors may be interested in loose affiliation when there is a strong digital or process platform to ensure efficiency in transactions.

The last strategy noted by Dee's et al is branching. Branching is basically setting up branches to spread your venture's reach. Branching is expensive but may also be essential for controlling the technical aspects of the

pp.24-32

product or business model. Investors may find branching important if there is the need for some control to protect the intellectual property.

Environental, Social and Governance (ESG)

Investors are increasingly looking at Environmental, Social and Governance (ESG) factors in making their investment decisions. Socially-conscious investors pay attention to the extent to which the venture adheres to these standards for operations. According to Investopedia[6], the Environmental criteria looks at how the venture performs as a steward of the natural environment. Social criteria examine how the venture manages relationships with its employees, suppliers, customers and the communities where it operates. Governance deals with the venture's leadership, executive pay, audits, internal controls and shareholder rights.

Some investors are increasingly looking for entrepreneurs that are "doing some good" while "doing well." They use a people and planet index to evaluate the entrepreneur's actions and the venture's business model. The bigger conversation is about hybridization. Analysts are using models such as the hybrid spectrum[7]to understand the extent to which ventures can blend social

---

6   https://bit.ly/2zVBOWg
7   Tom Reis, Unleashing New Resources and Entrepreneurship for the Common Good: A Scan, Synthesis, and Scenario for Action. W.K. Kellogg Foundation, January 1999. https://bit.ly/2M5MkRc

CHAPTER THREE

INNOVATING YOUR BUSINESS MODEL FOR INVESTMENT

Overview of Business Plan Development

A business plan is a road-map/plan that enables a business to analyse its past records and trends in the industry, project into the future, allocate resources, focus on key points, and prepare for challenges and opportunities that the business may face in the future.

Business plans are not just a fundraising document; they are far beyond that. They are vital for running the business, whether or not the business needs investments. A business plan helps you to think well in advance to mitigate any risk in the future. Businesses need plans to optimize growth and development according to priorities. If you want to build a competitive advantage, you must pay attention to efficiency, innovation, and creativity.

The structure of the business plan should vary based on where you want to use it. A business plan being created for fundraising should highlight a more detailed coverage of your current strengths and achievements which may not be required for a plan being made for internal planning. Make your plan match its purpose. Let's take a look at the structure of a typical business plan.

1.0 Executive Summmary

This a brief summary of the key elements of the business plan. It is supposed to be very catchy and attractive to readers. A good executive summary will compel an investor to read further to under the business model. The executive summary is supposed to be kept brief and presentable. It is advisable to use diagrams and graphs to entice whoever lays hands on the document and the content should be captured under the following headings.

1.1 Problem

1.2 Solution

1.3 Market

1.4 Competition

1.5 Financial Highlight

2.0 PROBLEM AND SOLUTION

You are supposed to write on the problem that has been identified in the society and explain the gap you are filling in the market. The problem must be easily understandable and one that people can relate to. It must also be worth solving and in the interest of the society.

The solution needs to be concise and very clear and scalable. Scalability is the capability of a system to increase its total output under an increased load when resources are added. This is what investors essentially want to see. They are interested in a company in which they can invest to have the wheel turn much faster. The content of this section can be captured under the following subsections.

2.1 Problem

2.2 Our Solution

2.3 Validation of Problem and Solution

2.4 Roadmap/Future Plans

3.0 MARKET ANALYS

The entrepreneur's understanding of the market size and needs is very important. At times entrepreneurs approach investors and tell them about untapped markets that they want to take advantage but do not actually know the size and how to capture it. The entrepreneur must know the market size and the opportunities available in the market that they want to tap. This is what the investor will evaluate to determine the potential return if he/she invests in your business.

Product screenshots and their description can also be added to this slide. Also, quotes of some of the existing customers talking about how much they love your product can be added.

3.1 Market Segmentation

3.2 Target Market Segment Strategy

3.3 Market Needs

3.4 Market Trends

3.5 Market Growth

3.6 Key Customer

3.7 Future Market

3.8 Competition

3.8.1 Competitors and Alternatives

3.8.2 Our Advantages

4.0 STRATEGY AND IMPLEMENTATION SUMMARY

This section must describe the rationale of how the company creates, delivers, and captures value. It must show action plans that specify how the company will reach customers and achieve competitive advantage. The section must also spell out the pricing and marketing strategy that the company will use to break into the market. Usually, when companies enter into the market, they create barriers to prevent new entrants; as such, it is good to spell out the strategy your company will pursue to break into the market and eventually get a larger market share.

It is good to indicate the stages in which the project will be monitored and measured for work performance. This provides the investor a clear picture of the execution of the project and the basis of measurement. As you may know, timing is everything in business and being at the right time in history is what really matters. Being too early or too late to market can be the main cause of failure for startups.

4.1 Product/Service

4.2 Marketing Plan

4.2 Sales Plan

4.3 Location and Facilities

4.4 Technology

4.5 Equipment and Tools

4.6 Milestones

4.7 Key Metrics

5.0 COMPANY AND MANAGEMENT SUMMARY

A brief history and the brains behind the establishment of the company is important at this point. The core management team is supposed to be included in the business plan with their profile. It is believed that a strong management team can be a driving force for businesses. A company that is solely managed may not compete effectively in the market as compared to a well-formed management team.

Also, it is good to indicate if the company has a board of directors or advisors. These people scrutinize the activities of the business, and it helps build investor confidence in the business. It also helps in decision-making. Investors are likely to invest in companies that have good governance structure.

5.1 Organisational Structure

5.2 Management Team

5.3 Management Team Gaps

5.4 Personnel Plan

5.5 Company History and Ownership

6.0 Financial Plan

Financial plan helps to determine how the business's strategic goals will be achieved. Performing financial planning is critical to the success of any organization and it is important to model the entire business through a spreadsheet/Excel model. Building a detailed spreadsheet model helps you plan your operational and financial decisions better – product development costs, expenses and business development plans, projections, working capital issues, cash flow issues, etc. get reflected best in a spreadsheet model.

6.1 Historical Financial Statements

6.2 Projected Financial Statements

6.2.1 Projected Profit or Loss

6.2.2 Projected Balance Sheet

6.2.3 Projected Cash flow Statement

6.2.4 Business Ratios

Feasibility Studies using BMC

Key Partners	Key Activities	Value Proposition	Customer Relationships	Customer Segments
Who are our key partners? Who are our key suppliers? Which key resources are we acquiring from partners? Which key activities do partners perform?	What key activities do our value propositions require? Our distribution channels? Customer relationships? Revenue streams?	What value do we deliver to the customer? Which one of our customer's problems are we helping to solve? What bundles of products and services are we offering to each customer	What type of relationship does each of our customer segments expect us to establish and maintain with them? Which ones have we established? How are they integrated with the rest of our business model? How costly are they?	For whom are we creating value? Who are our most important customers?

Key Resources	Key Pillars Positioning	Channels	Cost Structure	Revenue Streams
What key resources do our value propositions require? Our distribution channels? Customer relationships? Revenue streams?	Horizontal	Through which channels do our customer segments want to be reached? How are we reaching them now? How are our channels integrated? Which ones work best? Which ones are most cost-efficient? How are we integrating them with customer routines?	What are the most important costs inherent in our business model? Which ones have we established? Which key resources are most expensive? Which key activities are most expensive?	For what value are our customers really willing to pay? For what do they currently pay? How are they currently paying? How would they prefer to pay?

CHAPTER FOUR

DEVELOPING YOUR PITCH DECK

A pitch deck is a brief presentation in a PowerPoint format that an entrepreneur puts together to showcase his/ her business. A good pitch deck should be concise to attract the target. According to research conducted by DocSend, investors spend on average 3 minutes and 44 seconds per pitch deck. From their study which analyzed 200 pitch decks, investors spent the most amount of time reviewing the slides concerning financials, team, and competition.

An entrepreneur has to understand his/her business model very well and be able to communicate it to investors, customers and potential partners at any time. Whether the entrepreneur is pitching to a company, an investor, a customer, or a potential partner, he/she must hit them on both business and emotional levels and must know and understand their audience and tailor it accordingly.

It is also important to provide contact information on the last page of the pitch deck.

Below are the components of a good pitch deck. Each subtopic must be treated on a separate slide.

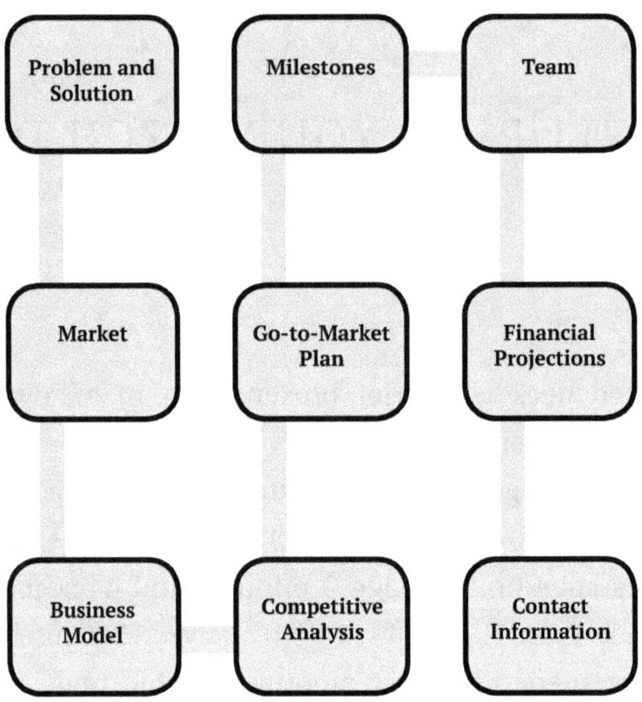

To begin with, it is important to have an interesting introduction in order to grab the audience's attention. Use images that directly relate to or complement what your company does, such as showing someone actively using your product or service, or the situation where someone would use it. The goal is to bring the audience 'into your world' here.

1. PROBLEM AND SOLUTION

The slide covering the problem should be a way for you to explain what gap you are filling in the market. The problem must be easily understandable and one that people can relate to. It must also be worth solving and in the interest of the society.

The solution needs to be concise, very clear, and scalable. Scalability is the capability of a system to increase its total output under an increased load when resources are added. This is what investors essentially want to see. They are interested in a company in which they can invest in order to have the wheel turn much faster.

Investors can only be interested in reading further because of the following reasons:

- They have experienced the same problem in the past
- There is a clear sense of return on investment down the line for them
- Given their professional expertise, they understand it

A good pitch deck must indicate the value the company will create to both the investor and society.

2. MARKET AND PRODUCT

The entrepreneur's understanding of the market size and needs is very important. At times entrepreneurs approach investors and tell them about untapped market that they want to take advantage but do not actually know the size and how to capture it. This is a common mistake that most entrepreneurs commit. The entrepreneur must know the market size and the opportunities available in the market that they want to tap. This is what the investor will evaluate to determine the potential return if he/she invests in your business.

Product screenshots and their descriptions can be added to this slide with quotes of some existing customers talking about how much they love your product.

It is recommended to show a graph that outlines the market growth in the past and the future potential growth so that investors can quantify the upside and potential return on investment if they invest. Ensure to include sources from research papers.

3. Business Model

This slide must describe the rationale of how the company creates, delivers, and captures value. Business model is a plan for the successful operation of a business, identifying sources of revenue, intended customers, key partners, products, and financing. This indicates clearly how the company will generate revenue and make profit.

4. MILESTONE

It is good to indicate the stages in which the project will be monitored and measured for work performance. This provides the investor a clear picture of the execution of the project and the basis of measurement.

5. GO-TO-MARKET PLAN

This slide should show an action plan that specifies how the company will reach customers and achieve competitive advantage. The purpose of a go-to-market is to provide a blueprint for delivering a product or service to customers taking into account factors such as pricing and distribution channels. This spells out the pricing and marketing strategy that the company will use to break into the market.

6. COMPETITION

A diagram is a good idea to show the investor the competitors executing in your space; how you compare with them and where you land with your value proposition.

You want to clearly differentiate yourself from the rest so that the person reviewing the slide gets what makes your company so unique. Understanding of your competitors' value proposition gives the investors the impression that you really understand your market and how your competitors are meeting customer expectations. Avoid statements referencing you being the only one doing this, you being the clear leader, etc. Just like Mark Cuban puts it, there are at least 100 people that have come up with that idea before you and other companies that may be tackling that same problem with a different approach.

7. TEAM

The team is probably one of the most important slides in any pitch deck. The investor wants to know those who are managing the business and what makes them so unique to execute on that mission and vision. The core management team is supposed to be included in the pitch deck with their profile. It is believed that a strong management team can be a driving force for businesses. A company that is solely managed may not compete effectively in the market as compared to a well formed management team.

The best way to showcase the team slide is by describing the members of the management team. List in bullet points what have been the two or three achievements from every member. Ideally, those would be related to the company that is seeking capital. Also, it is good to indicate if the company has a board of directors who scrutinize the activities of the business. Investors are likely to invest in companies that have good governance structure.

8. FINANCIALS

The company must provide a financial projection in the pitch deck and, if possible, a one- or two-year historical figure. These historical figures help investors to analyze the position of the company against the financial projections to assess its reasonableness. The entrepreneur must present a summary of 3-5 years' financial plan of the company. The number of years' financial projections to be presented in the pitch deck is largely influenced by the nature of the project the company will be undertaking. A 3-year financial plan may not be suitable for a project that is capital intensive in nature. This is because it will take a number of years for an investor to recoup his investment from such a project. As such, it will be better to provide more than 3 years financial projections; in this case, say, 5 years.

Even though projections are a shot in the dark when you are dealing with startups, they provide a good idea of where the business is heading and potential outcomes. It also gives a good idea to the investor as to how grounded the management of the company is. Investors are not interested in unrealistic projections, as such, you must get all your facts right and leave gap for no doubt. This slide is more important than entrepreneurs normally think. It is only summary of the financial projections that are needed at this point.

However, you must have readily available financial projections in an Excel format to be given to an investor upon request.

It is very important to state the amount that is needed to execute the business strategy in the pitch deck. It is also advisable to provide the breakdown in a diagram format.

How to Make a Good Pitch

- Be clear and concise to maintain interest
- Start with an elevator pitch – one or two lines that will capture their attention
- Be compelling – why should the investor buy in?
- Pay attention to details! Make sure presentation material is consistent and professional
- Do your research – know your target market, competitors, and audience to match their interests
- Be prepared – have the research and business plan to back up your claims
- Tell a story – everyone likes a compelling story and know your investor
- Talk about early successes – success in the past reduces risk for investors
- Have a thorough business plan in case the investor wants more details

- Be able to defend your projected financials

- Be prepared with known risks and mitigation strategies

55

CHAPTER FIVE

OTHER FUNDING OPTIONS

The sources of finance available to a company depend on several factors including financial position of the company, the financial risk, and the value of the company. Unless a company has a good financial position, several sources of finance may be unavailable. It is difficult to imagine a loss-making company which also has net liabilities being able to raise debt or equity finance successfully.

Similarly, a company with high level of financial gearing may not be able to raise additional debt finance due to the high level of financial risk. The value of a company will also make a difference to the types of finance that are available.

A company that has a higher value is more likely to attract providers of finance and be able to raise equity or debt finance.

PECKING ORDER

Pecking order theory states that a company will prefer retained earnings to any other source of finance and then choose debt and, last of all, equity. The order of preference will be: retained earnings, straight debt (bank loan), convertible debt, preference shares, and, lastly, equity.

Studies suggest that businesses that are most likely to follow pecking order theory operate profitably in the market where growth prospects are poor. There will, therefore, be limited opportunities to invest funds and these businesses will be content to rely on retained earnings for the limited resources that they need[1].

Funding Options

CROWDFUNDING

(GIFT-BASED AND EQUITY-BASED)

Crowdfunding is relatively a new trend of financing businesses at their early stage. It offers entrepreneurs the opportunity to raise money either in the form of gift or equity. This is done through online platforms focusing on social network. Crowdfunding is like posting a classified

---

[1] Reference
https://bit.ly/2JjuWKZ

advertisement on a website with the difference being that through crowdfunding sites, an entrepreneur can also advertise a business concept and request for funding from the crowd (Griffin, 2012). Kickstarter.com and kiva.com are examples of crowdfunding sites.

Crowdfunding is basically pitching a business idea to the general public and asking for donations to help bring your idea to reality. An entrepreneur can bypass the venture capitalists and angel investors and get directly in contact with regular internet users asking for small amounts of capital from many of them. Creators use certain websites such as kickstarter, indiegogo and kiva to pitch their ideas, business plans, product offerings, etc. and the investors in return are awarded in terms of discounts, free services or product offerings, once the company starts commercial operations (Scott Steinberg & Rusel deMaria, 2012).

Initially, the funding benefits to the investors were in the form of merchandize benefits but very recently, the concept of "Investment Crowdfunding" is coming up where the investors hold an ownership stake in the new business in the form of equity known as "Equity Crowdfunding" or receive interest payments from the entrepreneur known as "Debt Crowdfunding." The concept of gift-based (donation) can also not be overemphasized. Gift-based (Donations) involves philanthropies donating funds mostly for charities and non-profit organizations. Profit organizations can also receive donations through this medium. Donation is considered to be one of the widely spread forms of crowdfunding.

According to Manchanda and Muralidharan (2014), crowdfunding can act as a marketing tool for a start-up firm as it increases product or brand awareness among the general public. One gets to test and prove the popularity of the model. Also, it provides genuine feedback regarding the idea and if the funding received is nowhere close to the target capital, the idea must be given another thought. In the case of basic crowdfunding where equity is not transferred, the cost is almost zero. They argued that there is always a fear of loss of confidentiality as the idea is shared with many others and a risk of the idea being stolen and implemented before the pioneer does. Additionally, a lot of time and effort is required to promote an idea through campaigns and promotions.

Angel investors are wealthy individuals who invest in start-up and growth businesses in return for an equity stake. The investment can involve both time and money depending on the investor. These individuals are prepared to take high risks in the hope of high returns. As a result, angel investors' finance can be expensive for the business.

Angel Investors

Angel investors are very useful to fill the gap between venture capital and debt finance, particularly for startup businesses. One of the main advantages of angel investors is that they often follow up their initial investment with later rounds of financing as the business grows. New businesses benefit from their expertise in the difficult early stages of trying to establish themselves.

Angel investing of this sort has existed for centuries, but, over the past couple of decades, the angel investment sector has gained increasing recognition as a powerful source of financing for high-growth companies and has become more formalized and organized, including syndicates, associations, and networks (Ibrahim, 2008; OECD, 2011a).

Individual Control And Investment

As hinted earlier, the discussion around funding is often focused on high growth space. However, there are some concerns relating to individual control that influences how entrepreneurs relate to investors. There are different types of entrepreneurs and their individual control profile may explain how they approach funding. For instance, entrepreneurs with high individual control needs may choose to become lifestyle entrepreneurs or small business owners. Entrepreneurs with low individual control needs are more likely to be the high growth entrepreneur, serial entrepreneur or some franchise entrepreneur. Further, the lower individual control needs, the higher the preference for equity; and the higher individual control needs, the lower a preference for equity.

Of course, there could also be hybrid-control entrepreneurs. For instance, those who like control but are able to build large businesses organically because they are either really good or their ideas are really good.

Recognition has come with more regulation, although the angel investing market is largely informal, i.e. BAs act privately and generally prefer to maintain anonymity (CSES, 2012).

In the US, angel investors need approval as "accredited investors" under securities laws, whereas in other countries certification is necessary but can take the form of a self-certification. These requirements are intended to ensure that the investors have the necessary financial resources as well as an understanding of the implications of investing in start-up companies (OECD, 2011a).[2]

IMPACT INVESTMENT

Business activities were formerly regarded as a problem for the environmental movement but the two are now increasingly complimentary and both investors and business owners are making gradual effort to improve social and economic life of the society in which they operate. The business environment is now witnessing a new paradigm of investment called impact investment. Impact investors look out for businesses that are not financial return-oriented but also the environmental, social and governance of the business. Bugg-Levine and Emerson (2011) argued that these investors and the strategies they are executing are the early signs of a long-forming undercurrent poised to reshape how society deploys its resources and solves its problems. Impact

2   Reference
    Scott Steinberg, Rusel deMaria (2012) "The Crowd Funding Bible," published by Read. me, May,
        p. 1-90
    Griffin, Z.J (2012). CrowdFunding: Fleecing the American Masses. Forthcoming in Case Western Reserve Journal of Law, Technology & the Internet.
    Karish Manchanda, Pushkala Muralidharan(2014), Crowdfunding: A New Paradigm In Startup Financing, Global conference on business and finance proceedings, volume 9, no. 1

investment is another way philanthropies can deploy their resources and achieve their goal whiles generating some financial return.

Impact investments are investments made into companies, organizations, and funds with the intention to generate social and environmental impact alongside a financial return. Impact investments can be made in both emerging and developed markets, and target a range of returns from below market to market rate, depending on investors' strategic goals.

The growing impact investment market provides capital to address the world's most pressing challenges in sectors such as sustainable agriculture, renewable energy, conservation, microfinance, and affordable and accessible basic services including housing, healthcare, and education.

Characteristics Of Impact Investing

GIIN maintained that the practice of impact investing is further defined by the following four core characteristics:

Intentionality: An investor's intention to have a positive social or environmental impact through investments is essential to impact investing.

Investment with Return Expectations: Impact investments is expected to generate a financial return on capital or, at minimum, a return of capital.

<u>Range of Return Expectations and Asset Classes:</u> Impact investments target financial returns that range from below market (sometimes called concessionary) to risk-adjusted market rate, and can be made across asset classes, including but not limited to cash equivalents, fixed income, venture capital, and private equity.

<u>Impact Measurement:</u> A hallmark of impact investing is the commitment of the investor to measure and report the social and environmental performance and progress of underlying investments, ensuring transparency and accountability while informing the practice of impact investing and building the field.

Investors' approaches to impact measurement will vary based on their objectives and capacities, and the choice of what to measure usually reflects investor goals and, consequently, investor intention. Some of the key factors that impact investors look out for include: number of jobs created (poverty alleviation), number of women employed and are in strategic positions of the company, use of environmentally-friendly equipment and social activities engaged in by the company.

REASONS FOR IMPACT INVESTING

Impact investing challenges the long-held views that social and environmental issues should be addressed only by philanthropic donations, and that market investments should focus exclusively on achieving financial returns.

The impact investing market offers diverse and viable opportunities for investors to advance social and environmental solutions through investments that also produce financial returns.

Many types of investors are entering the growing impact investing market. Here are a few common investor motivations:

- Banks, pension funds, financial advisors, and wealth managers can provide client investment opportunities to both individuals and institutions with an interest in general or specific social and/or environmental causes.

- Institutional and family foundations can leverage significantly greater assets to advance their core social and/or environmental goals while maintaining or growing their overall endowment.

- Government investors and development finance institutions can provide proof of financial viability for private-sector investors while targeting specific social and environmental goals.

- Impact investment can be in a form of interest-free loan or interest rate that is below market interest rate. It can also take the form of equity or grant.[3]

---

3   Reference
    GIIN   https://thegiin.org/impact-investing/   need-to-know/   #core-characteris-tics-of-impact-investing
    Emerson, A. B.-L. (2011). Impact Investing, Transforming How We Make Money. Hoboken, New Jersey: John Wiley & Sons.

www.ingramcontent.com/pod-product-compliance
Lightning Source LLC
Chambersburg PA
CBHW050604160726
48003CB00003B/1050